#IMPACT

BECAUSE IT'S NOT JUST ABOUT THE LIPSTICK

Redefining Success in the
Beauty Retail Industry in a
Time of Disruption.

BECKY FEELEY

DISCLAIMER

#IMPACT - BECAUSE IT'S NOT JUST ABOUT THE LIPSTICK

Published by Fig Factor Media, LLC.
Printed in the United States of America
Cover Design and Layout by Juan Pablo Ruiz

FIG FACTOR MEDIA

The opinions expressed in our published works are those of the author(s) and do not reflect the opinions of Fig Factor Media or its Editors.

ISBN: 978-1-952779-02-2
Library of Congress Number: 2020942619

This book is dedicated to my mentor, Gigi Kane, who shows strength and courage while leading with grace. Thank you, Gigi, for never giving up on me.

CONTENTS:

———

FORWARD

To the lucky reader,

If you are beginning your career in cosmetic retail, congratulations! You are about to embark on the most exciting and rewarding journey. If you are seasoned in the industry, congratulations as well! It takes tremendous hard work, passion, purpose, and resilience to get where you are today.

Over the past nine years, there is no one I have known to wear as many hats, stand in as many shoes, and mentor as many people as Rebecca Feeley. From behind the counter, to a mom of three, and executive level boss in many different roles, she has been recognized for inspiring countless individuals to create high touch experiences that serve a bigger purpose.

In this book, Becky shares tested, proven, and honest feedback that will help you to hit the ground running. But more importantly, she will inspire you, as she did to me, to ignite your inner purpose. Because being a beauty advisor is more than just about lipstick.

-Kayla McAndrews

Field Executive, ELC Portfolio. Indianapolis, IN

INTRODUCTION

———

When I first started writing this book, I wanted to inform every reader on how to be successful in the cosmetic retail industry. Then COVID-19 appeared in all our lives like a TON OF BRICKS. Everything has changed.

The word "furlough" is now commonplace in our vocabulary. The people that haven't felt the direct impact that this pandemic has had over our lives will find out sooner than later.

Life, death, safety, and the economy are impacting our lives and turning it into a journey that no one living has experienced before. I have had sleepless nights where I am unsure how my life, family, and career will survive. Suddenly, I realized it is time to share my story as we discover every day who we really are, and what we really stand for in this world. This book explores our emotional intelligence by learning our SELF intelligence first. I am ready to take that journey with you, and together we will not only survive all the changes, but we will thrive by redefining what success means to us.

Throughout my 20-year retail career in the beauty industry, I've had thousands of conversations with customers resulting in millions of dollars' worth of products. I majored in fashion merchandising but managing clothing in a large department store turned into a promotion to assistant manager of cosmetics. From then on, beauty was in my blood. My career flourished as I stepped into more positions in the beauty retail industry, such as:

Department Manager of Cosmetics, Human Resource Manager, Store Management, Beauty Advisor, Counter Manager, Freelance Makeup Artist, National Makeup Artist, Midwest Account Coordinator, and Cosmetic Executive for a Fortune 500 Beauty Brand. The connections I've made throughout the years have both enriched my life and the lives of my customers. This is #IMPACT up close and personal.

YOU ARE THE KEY TO IT ALL.

Changes in thought or behavior are not always easy. The journey of trial and error represent transition and growth. As specific as merchandising is as a business practice, and as abstract as our life purpose seems to be for all of us, keep your mind open as you read. This book is designed to grow with you as your profession highlights specific things you want to always remember to look back on in your career. Grab a notebook and journal your thoughts as you answer the questions throughout this book. Circumstances and goals change and grow over time, therefore reevaluate when you feel it's necessary. As nerve wracking and scary a time this is, I am confident that this book will take you to the next level of self-discovery.

As a new world emerges, there is not a better time than now to embrace all your past experiences and realize how they have impacted your life and others. I want you to recognize all the gifts that you have to give. How we were defined before has shifted. You are here for a reason and you are meant to live a life of purpose and happiness -- no matter what is happening in the world around us. Do not procrastinate. Share your passion and help others with what you have learned throughout your life. You ARE ready to move to the next level and once you open yourself up to the vulnerability of sharing your stories, there will be a sense of fulfillment. When we search for more of anything, this is the signal that it is time to go a step further in our lives and step out of our box. As you try new things, self-discovery unfolds, and it leads us to places we could never imagine. I always say, "If it were easy then everyone would do it." Nothing worthwhile or significant is ever easy but action is the key when breaking through barriers. It takes courage to tell your story and describe what lives in your heart as you conquer challenges. Your experiences will help others while it opens doors to learn even more. Open your heart as we learn though the shifting of the world and your actions show deliberate effort in moving forward for a more fulfilled and purposeful life.

Relationships are everything and the gift of human touch will never be taken for granted anymore. We need...each other.

During unpredictable times, trying new things will ultimately result in success. Right now, every day is unpredictable. We are traveling in unchartered territories. There will always be disruptions and events that will create instability. We do not have control over our surroundings, but we do have control on how we act and react. This is the time to keep learning and pushing yourself to the limits of what you can accomplish. Do not sit back and wait for the world to tell you what your future holds.

This is a no-judgement, unbiased, emotion-FULL, and STORY-FULL book that is written for YOU. Years of experience and situations are documented that will help clear the dust on questions of direction. Let's discover what BEAUTY means to you as we travel through a journey of self-discovery to provide an even bigger impact in the cosmetic industry.

XO,

-Becky Feeley

1

YOU ARE THE KEY TO IT ALL

YOU are the most integral part of developing, maintaining, and growing a business. Without customers a business could not survive. As the person servicing the customer, you are the one who delivers the message.

The beauty industry consists of both products and services that are critical to the modern economy. Like many service industries, we create loyal customers by building relationships through connection. During the COVID-19 pandemic, it became obvious that humans crave physical and emotional contact with people that digital technology cannot provide. Social distancing can be an emotional rollercoaster. Some great days we feel tremendous gratitude while other days there are feelings of sadness, frustration, and fear. Retail will never be the same, but with understanding, hope, and adaptability we will become stronger as a community.

SUCCESS LIVES INSIDE YOU

The way we will begin to overcome this retail apocalypse is by understanding the past before we can start to rebuild for the future. Trust your instinct. Allow yourself to use your best judgement to make decisions. Guidance is a gift but honor your opinion and speak your truth. Your talents will shine, and your value will soar when you give yourself permission to let go of the cookie cutter mold and start creating a bigger vision. By following the mold, and without giving your value and input, you become replaceable. Anyone can follow a recipe, but the magic will happen when you add the personal touch.

In the service industry, our focus is always on everyone else. We are consumed by making our customers, our boss(es), and our co-workers happy. Take the time to understand what motivates you while feeling a sense of fulfillment. Confidence and purpose can lead you to success without the weight of the world or redundancy.

I want you to give yourself a break and take the pressure off. You will always rise above the ashes. Perseverance shows strength against all odds, and that is what will continue to feed business growth. Your strength and self-discoveries are key to finding your purpose while helping others.

Two things that will be repeated throughout this book are:

1) Your efforts match your success

2) Never. Give. Up.

Where do you even begin, you ask? Find YOUR why and live with a sense of fulfillment. Many employees in the service industry have not realized the extreme influence they have on people. A simple connection, application, or knowledge that we take for granted can change someone's mood, confidence, and even future. We are teachers, we are friends, we are significant, and we are here to create personal experiences to make people FEEL as beautiful as they are.

Your efforts will never go unnoticed, no matter what your position. Feel proud to take this time to take a step back and invest in yourself. The complexities of emotion that go along with beauty services represent the power of self-care and expression. It is time to break down barriers and open our hearts to embrace the #IMPACT.

Grab a notebook. You'll find three DIFFERENT TIERS OF DISCOVERY throughout this book. They will help you activate your #IMPACT in measurable ways.

- Beginners: new to the industry
- Seasoned: an experienced employee
- Leaders: management roles of any kind

YOUR STORY MATTERS

I believe in the power of telling your personal stories. As an executive, bullet points are necessary for efficiency; however, a story brings a message to life. A story is visualizing and relating to what a person is saying. Stories inspire visualization, relational connections, and the potential to provoke thought. The service industry is unique, and new situations arise in it every day. I believe in personalization, creativity, and the freedom to connect through a story, while learning through others. As I tell my personal stories, you should reflect on your own experiences and how they have shaped who you are today. Your story provides value to YOU first, then others.

ACTIVATION IS KEY

I am confident that you are on your way to make a greater impact on yourself and others. As results are never guaranteed, always remember that activation is the key. New actions may feel awkward but understand that this is a feeling of learning.

Feel confident that you have a "home" in this ever-changing world of cosmetic and beauty retail - but it will take hard work, persistence, and consistency. A growth mindset will make you unstoppable and when you never give up, opportunities will appear. A life of fulfillment, gratitude, and purpose will drive you to succeed in a career filled with beauty. Positivity to move forward will feed your stamina, resilience, and ability to thrive under any condition. If the world puts you on stand-by, then get on another flight.

#IMPACT

2

SUCCESS, REDEFINED

———

Your priorities will change as time passes. Your plans will go right down the drain as the unexpected arises. Dreams shift as life experience gives perspective of what is important and where life's journey takes you. With that said, please know you are here for a reason and it is important to celebrate each day. Whether it is thriving or surviving, twists and turns create strength and resilience. They build our life narrative.

Your story makes you beautiful, unique, and significant. Prioritize what is important to you and take action. "You can have it all, just not all at once," wrote Oprah Winfrey. Here's a story about career, babies, love, and perseverance.

OWN YOUR DECISIONS

In 2006, my career was on an upswing. I was an account coordinator managing six stores for a cosmetic brand while enjoying freedom with my handsome husband, Tim. I had interviewed for an education executive position with my company but ended up not getting it. At the time, I felt fantastic even interviewing for an executive position, because to me, this would be in my near future. As a merchandise management major at the International Academy of Merchandising and Design in Chicago, it was my ultimate goal to become an executive within a large corporation to positively impact the retail industry. Tim had a bright future in front of him as well, starting his career for one of the largest banks in the world. We do not come from wealthy parents, but we come from good parents that worked for every penny that they have, so we do the same. Work was always top priority as we started building our future together.

Amid this carefree and career driven life, I had baby fever. I wanted to start a family YESTERDAY. When my mind is set on something, I tend to go after it obsessively. What I did not realize at the time, was that God laughs at our plans and life turns out the way it is meant to be. After four unsuccessful months, I headed to the fertility doctor and exaggerated that I had been trying to get pregnant for one year. I had done my homework and found out that fertility specialists prefer patients under thirty-five years old to try for twelve months before a consultation. Honestly, I just wanted one of those magic pills that would make me pregnant right away so I could move on with my life. I had my nanny all set (my mother) and worked out my back-to-work regimen with this baby that only existed in my mind and heart.

I had life completely planned, balanced, and strategically figured out. Wow was I surprised at what happened next.

After all the tests were complete at the fertility center, I was informed that I had an adenoma (tumor) on my pituitary gland in my brain. This gland controls hormones and was keeping me from conceiving. Surgery was not necessary yet, but medicine was needed to shrink the tumor before I started any fertility treatments. Nothing was guaranteed. My days turned into feelings of dismay and a constant lump in my throat ready to cry at any given moment. Since starting a family was my primary focus, there were kids and pregnant ladies everywhere I turned. It almost felt like there was some sort of baby boom! Oh, and the baby showers...

As my first round of medication started, Tim and I went for dinner at a nearby steakhouse. I had on a sparkly baby blue tank top from BEBE, jeans, and silver t-strap stilettos. We sat in a booth in the corner, and tears just started streaming down my face. No sound of whimpers, just tears flowing as I looked at my husband preparing what to say. "I am not sure if I am able to have children. I know how important starting a family is to you, and I give my support to move on with your life without me." As I saw Tim's sweet face turn teary eyed, he got up, sat next to me in the booth.

Holding me tight he said, "I will stand with you forever, no matter what. I am never leaving you."

Our paychecks went entirely to the fertility doctor and I was in a daze by all the medication. For 16 months, every morning I drove Tim to the train for work and together we would pray a novena to St. Gerard, Patron Saint of Pregnant Women. I took a step down from my job for more flexibility between doctor appointments and I did not have to travel. During the fertility treatments, I was also treating the pituitary tumor. To shrink the tumor, I was taking medication that would eventually be discontinued when/if we conceived. Physical side effects included hot flashes and extreme fatigue, but it was the emotional distress of every negative pregnancy test that took the biggest toll.

In 2007, after exhausting all options, we eventually opted to move forward with in vitro fertilization (IVF). A huge box of medication arrived at our door, and I used it all in three weeks. Patches, pills, and injections prepared me for the procedure. I looked and felt six months pregnant by the time I went in for the doctor to retrieve my eggs. About five days later, Tim and I completed the process by going back into the fertility center. The doctor came into the room while we were waiting for the embryo transfer (basically where they insert an embryo and hope it turns into a viable pregnancy).

"Great news." The doctor said. "You have 15 beautiful

embryos and there are two that we have graded as A++. This means they are essentially perfect. We can either transfer one or both. If we transfer both, then your chances of conceiving increase dramatically, however so does the chances of having twins. You are young and healthy, so one could do the trick. Let me give you a few minutes to decide privately."

The doctor walked out of the room, and Tim and I blankly looked at each other while I was in my white surgical gown. Thoughts raced through our minds. What should we do? We were certain of two things. First, I did not know how much more I could take physically and emotionally. Second, we both knew this was our only chance due to finances. We had spent all our money on fertility treatments and we tapped out our insurance. It was decided.

Seven months later we gave birth to premature twin boys. It was a tough pregnancy, and I was on bed rest from 15 weeks on due to my small frame. I had a pump in my leg feeding me medication 24 hours a day to help stop premature labor, but nothing compared to the non-stop worry when my boys were in the hospital for eight weeks after their birth. The boys had some struggles as they grew, but they were strong and healthy. My pituitary tumor continued to be controlled by medication and still is to this day.

Surprises kept coming when I naturally became pregnant

with our daughter 18 months later! Every day was a journey of gratitude through the unexpected. What I was sure of was that my "plan" of working full-time after my magic pill baby was born was completely out the window.

We were BROKE.

Broke in the sense that I could not work more than 6 hours a week with 3 babies under 3. Tim made too much to qualify for any government assistance programs, but we had enough to pay our mortgage and a whopping $50 for weekly groceries. We survived thanks to my Aunt and Uncle bringing us meals and baby formula every week. We had a minivan that needed to take a "rest" for about an hour if I stopped the engine. My Mom started a "preschool fund" for the twins where she would contribute $20 a week in a labeled envelope in our kitchen. Financially, we were a wreck. As a family, we were complete. I saw all my children take their first steps and heard their first words.

I was able to volunteer at all the school functions and never missed a sports game. Eventually, we went from broke to comfortable on a strict budget. Some people judged me for not working and sacrificing financial freedom to stay at home with our kids. It was a humbling and simple time in my life, and it was MY decision.

Due to timing and circumstances when the boys were about eight, I went back to work full-time and full force. People then judged when I focused on my career and did not volunteer as much at their school. Holy cow, you can't win sometimes! It was a time to rediscover who I was and face the truth: It was MY decision.

Here is the thing. There will be people that will cheer you on from the sidelines no matter what, and people that will negatively judge your decisions, NO MATTER WHAT. Say Sayonara to the judges, embrace your supporters, and feel proud to make YOUR OWN DECISIONS!

HEY, GRATITUDE, YOU ARE EVERYTHING

I'm giving you this straight: Gratitude will get you through any challenging situation.

Priorities will change with what your heart desires and what is most important to you. What may seem like a step back and confusing to other people, will leave you feeling confident in your decisions.

When things don't work out as planned, be grateful.

Many people assumed that my company asked me to step down, and they could not grasp that I would do this voluntarily. At first it bothered me that people were even thinking I wasn't performing "enough" to stay in my position, but I knew exactly what I was doing.

When you realize you are not defined by others, be grateful.

Stay true to who you are and do not make decisions based on what people may think of you or their definition of success. Define your own success. If you feel unsure of what to do, pray about it. Clarity will come.

When you feel uncertain (I promise, you won't stay there forever!), be grateful.

SELF-CARE, SELF-LOVE

You are in the service industry and it is in your nature to put people's needs in front of your own. The concern and thoughtfulness of others is a gift to the world, but keep in mind that you cannot care for others to its fullest potential unless you take care of yourself first. The health of you and your family is the most important factor in happiness. Support yourself, support others, and allow people to support you.

Own your decisions. Be grateful. Take care of yourself. These are the first steps to redefining success. No matter where you are in your journey, I know with 100 percent certainty that you are on your way to making a greater impact on yourself and others. Onto the many levels of YOU . . .

3

SIX BEST PRACTICES AT EVERY LEVEL

———

There are dozens of layers to Mother Earth. Each one has its own characteristics and composition. There are different levels to us too: skin-deep, emotional, relationships with others, our personal life, and our professional life. That's why, when we talk about the extraordinary world of the beauty industry, it's not just about the lipstick!

LEVEL 1: HOME IS WHERE THE HEART IS

I received the best advice when I started back to work full time. As I was about to embark as an executive, I was told, "First and foremost, make sure you take care of your home and the people in it. Once you know you are leaving with everything as put together as you possibly can, your job will reflect that. You will be calmer, more efficient, and your focus will improve. Take the time to take care of your home. Do not feel guilty as you will be a better employee because of it."

A story about a supermarket deli line may seem like a silly choice for a book on success in the beauty industry-- but I think about this story every day because it speaks to how redefining success begins at home.

I was shopping in our local grocery store and I was crabby. Honestly, I have no idea what I was crabby about, and for whatever reason I was incredibly annoyed in general. I took a number from the deli and there were a few people in front of me. My husband called and asked me to pick up something he needed while I was at the store. I mumbled grumpily and sarcastically snapped back at him that "of course" I will get him anything he needs because I have all the time in the world to take care of everyone.

Do you ever have these days? And sometimes for no reason! I hung up the phone, rolled my eyes, and then my deli number was called. I looked up and smiled at the clerk behind the counter and pleasantly ordered my sliced turkey and ham. It was such a pleasant exchange that I started to think, why in the world would I be more pleasant to a stranger than the people that I love and love me the most? That really isn't fair, is it?

I remember this story when there are long days at work and it is my job to be pleasant, smile, and provide positive experiences to my team and customers. There are tough days. Long days. But home is truly where the heart is. Treat your loved ones even better than anyone you meet in this world. If you have a rough day, then have a grateful heart for those around you and make sure that you do not take out your frustrations on them. As you would go to work and leave any personal issues at the door, provide the same respect in your home. Leave your job at work.

LEVEL 2: INCLUSIVITY AND THE WORLD AROUND YOU

Consistency in your actions apply to everyone that you work with and service daily. Unless you have walked in someone's shoes, you truly do not understand what they have been through or are going through. Inclusivity is more than just good intentions. It is educating yourself on how to be an ally to those around you of different ethnicities, cultures, and lifestyles. Ask questions. Be informed. Do not assume. Support. Activate.

Personally, I have been unintentionally biased with actions I thought were purposely inclusive. You are a good person, but to truly be an ally, it means to put all defensiveness off the table and decide to take action. Listen to understand, not to respond. Educate to activate what is right for equality.

Beginners, Seasoned, and Leaders:

I suggest taking an online class or research on how to truly practice inclusion. It improves personal and team engagement that promotes a healthy workplace. Find your outlet to educate and practice inclusivity. If you work in the beauty industry, it is a priority that you feel confident and capable of serving all ethnicities with the correct products tailored to them. This is non-negotiable.

Black, Beautiful, and Empowered

I asked Nia Burgess, a good friend and talented aesthetician in Chicago, her opinion on how beauty industry professionals can exhibit inclusivity in the black community and beyond. She has hosted open Q&A on social media about what it truly means to be an ally and has experienced social injustice as a black woman. I consider her forthright, honest, and cultured.

Nia opened up and told me her story on how she decided to start a career in the beauty industry. "At age 15, my mom took me to get matched for a foundation at a store in Highland, Indiana, where I grew up. A beauty professional, and I say that loosely, started helping me and was having difficulty matching my skin. She ended up matching me to a color that literally looked gray. She suggested that I should not apply it all over so I wouldn't look completely gray. I not only knew that I wanted a career in beauty, but at that moment, I knew I had to."

What is discouraging is that there are still people that work in the beauty industry that do not feel confident or comfortable matching all skin tones. Specific colors are chosen of eyeshadow, blush, and lipstick based on how light or dark someone's skin is. To say this is unacceptable is an understatement. Every single person should feel confident to be serviced the same, no matter what. Everyone deserves expertise and knowledge from any beauty professional getting paid to be an expert. It is your job to educate yourself on the craft of makeup, not the craft of makeup for some people. Nia is a gift to this world because she has made it her life focus to help educate the artistry world on the skills necessary for true and authentic inclusivity.

Nia and I continued to discuss that service is not brand biased, and true servicing is not just offering one specific brand, but the best products for each individual. Knock down those invisible brand walls, and always be honest with yourself and others.

Would you like to dance?

I have also learned from the wise words of my good friend, Tamika Lychee Morales, founder of The Autism Hero Project. Tamika opened my eyes, and eyes of many others, when we were doing a virtual event called, "Conquer with Community" during the Covid-19 pandemic. The event was about empowering others and making sure people knew they were not alone during such an uncertain time. Tamika created her awareness by saying the analogy, "Inclusion is more than just inviting someone to the party. It is asking them to dance, meeting them where they are, and creating space for them. Everyone wins with inclusion because everyone learns."

No one on this Earth is exactly alike, and our differences elevate us as individuals. The sense of belonging is a basic need in the human brain and translates into feeling safe and valued. The workplace should never feel like a popularity contest. Make efforts purposeful and it will speak volumes of your character.

LEVEL 3: YOUR COWORKERS

If you have been in this industry for more than a few minutes, you are familiar with "the lines in the sand." It is where cosmetic salespeople could feel "territorial" and do not want anyone else to sell their product. The only acceptable way they would agree with anyone helping with their brand, is if you ring it for them so they can get the commission. Otherwise, other associates selling "their products" are taking "their customers."

This is an old way of thinking. We need to create business by personal relationships and connections, and if someone is bringing a customer over that they have connected with, be THANKFUL. It is helping your brand and keeping business in the building. When you keep business in the building, hours or positions are less likely to decrease and doors stay open. Our co-workers are our allies. Build relationships not only with your customers but with each other.

If you need help, it comes with *initiating* help. It is not about what people can do for you, but what you can do for people. When you initiate the reciprocation, you will get back ten times what you give. That is the beauty of it. In layman's terms, if you help others, others will help you. This is a time when we need each other to succeed. Some healthy competition may be fun, but at the end of the day, if everyone wins, we all win. Do not try and "outperform" your co-workers, try to "outperform" yourself. Let's keep those doors open together.

Help your coworkers, collaborate, cooperate, and go the extra mile to "educate so we don't vacate."

LEVEL 4: YOUR SENSE OF WONDER AND INSPIRATION

This is your drive that keeps you going. We all get tired but sometimes we need a kick in the butt to keep moving. I love quotes of inspiration to give me a quick jolt of energy that is better than an espresso shot. Whether you find them on Google or Instagram, one will inspire you and suddenly you will hop back on your feet ready to go!

A few of my favorite inspirational quotes are:

"Champions aren't made in gyms. Champions are made from something they have deep inside them—a desire, a dream, a vision. They have to have the skill AND the will. But the will must be stronger than the skill." - Muhammad Ali

"Luck is a dividend of sweat. The more you sweat, the luckier you get." - Ray Kroc

"If you do what you've always done, you'll get what you've always gotten." - Tony Robbins

Beginners: Your skills probably have not fully developed yet. Your efforts of learning and discovering what works for you and what doesn't is the most powerful tool you have. Mentors can be so powerful at this stage and you are on the path to master your craft. You will learn what gets you out of bed in the morning and what kind of person you want to be known for.

Seasoned: The espresso shot of daily inspiration is a necessity at this point. You are at risk of becoming stagnant and in this world today you must continue to embrace the changing landscape all around us. Consistency in quality effort paves the way for the rest of those around you.

Leaders: During change you should create the innovation or inspire and execute your team's innovation. Be open to new ideas and always recognize the effort. Do not be fooled by initial results that may take time to evolve and turn into something significant. Innovators are a gift because they feed energy and provide solution-oriented passion that is contagious.

LEVEL 5: DESTINATION ADDICTION

I will be truly happy when…
I will be so much happier when I…
My life will be so much better when…

Destination addiction is the mindset that happiness is somewhere other than the present. I have not only experienced these same feelings in my own life, but I have seen others have these thoughts as well. It is always good to strive for new goals, but when it distracts you from the present is when it stops you from appreciating the life you have right now. I am a firm believer that abundance comes when we appreciate and are grateful for the here and now.

Waiting for things to happen is a trap. At the end of each individual day, reflect on the impact you had and what you accomplished. It doesn't have to be huge, just if you can think of *something, anything,* that made you feel accomplished. This changes during different times in life. I have days when I go to bed knowing I gave my best effort and made a difference in someone's life. Other days it could be just survival during a difficult time. Let steps towards progress--not perfection--be your compass and give yourself credit for every step forward you accomplish along the way.

I will always remember this talented employee who aspired to be promoted into a very high leadership position. Every couple of weeks she would ask for my opinion about a job that she saw online. Eventually I told her to stop looking on LinkedIn and start putting that energy into her job performance. This is when a position would come to her, not the other way around. Her eyes ended up opening, learning from those who supported her, and I saw her newfound freedom as she tried new things. Sure enough, eight months later she was promoted while elevating herself along the way.

There is a difference between starting an entirely new career or looking for a new job. A new career is something entirely different than what you are doing currently, whereas a new job is simply staying in the same industry but looking to join another company. I have seen many people searching for fulfillment and unhappy in a position for many reasons, but the key to your happiness lies only within you. There will be challenges in any position and nothing will ever be perfect. Later in the book we will discuss how the beauty industry is a small, big world, but for now I will quote my authentic and talented friend Hiba Shire, who said, "A company that aligns with your values and purpose while caring for their employees is priceless."

LEVEL 6: YOU ARE YOUR BRAND

There is a difference between FEEDBACK and CRITICISM. Feedback should be encouraged; criticism is unwanted advice.

The definition of perception: A thought, belief, opinion, often held by many people and based on appearances. -dictionary. cambridge.org

As part of self-discovery, ask yourself how you make people feel. This is much different than people's judgments about you. Take a step back in situations and ask yourself how you are making people feel by your actions. We are put on this Earth to be kind to one other and try to understand perceptions to better ourselves.

Feedback is an opinion that is not about being right or wrong, it is sharing an opinion or feeling. I am sure you have heard the saying "think before you speak," and this just takes it to the next level. Before you speak or act, what kind of reactions are you looking for? Are you acting in a way that will better yourself and other people? Are you being true to your values? Is what you say made to make people feel guilty, pressured, or ashamed? Or are your words or actions open, positive, humble, and patient? Your "brand" reflects people's perception of you.

My coworker Danette Reisner, gave me the advice, "You want people to look forward to your visit, not having them count down the minutes until you leave."

My feeling is that if you are sincere, authentic, and genuinely a good person, your "brand" will speak for itself.

4

LEARNING WILL NEVER GO TO WASTE

———

Can you think of a specific time that perhaps seemed like a failure or disappointment but ended up being a blessing in disguise? When you felt an urge or longing to pursue something?

Do not resist! Keep listening to that voice inside you and make sure you trust yourself enough to make efforts in achieving whatever may be in your heart. All your efforts and hard work will ALWAYS be worth it. Don't rely solely on my words of advice, TRUST YOURSELF.

ANGELS IN DISGUISE

When I was at home with my three children under six years old, I came up with another "plan" of going back to school to become a nurse. My plan consisted of working 12-hour shifts, three nights a week at Edward Hospital in Naperville, Illinois, to earn a salary while being able to have my days with the kids. My mother was a nurse specializing in Memory Care for over 50 years, and she encouraged the idea. I signed up at College of DuPage to update my science courses, become a Certified Nurse's Assistant (CNA), and start my journey.

I loved school. Going to college later in life has a completely different connotation. This time I was intrigued by every new piece of information I learned and valued my time "away" during study groups. The first day I started my CNA course, I sat next to this very chatty young girl. Maddie was about twenty years old, a cute girl with short brown hair. The minute I smiled at her and introduced myself, she immediately started telling me stories about her friends and why she was inspired to become a nurse. Maddie told me all about her high school days and how she helped take care of her friends with special needs. Sometimes her chattiness was distracting, but nonetheless, I enjoyed her stories. Little did I know what an important person she would be in my life.

Maddie took care of my sweet grandmother the last two years of her life. She was the angel our family needed and I am forever grateful that our lives connected. My mother was able to do most of the heavy lifting, but Maddie ended up being a very special companion to my "Gran". She loved Maddie's chatty nature and looked forward to her visits. Maddie if you are reading this, I want you to know how much your kind heart meant to us during such a difficult time of loss and heartache.

After our certification was completed, a new sense of accomplishment came over me more than it ever had before. I was asked to represent in the college website video, advertising the Certified Nurse's Assistant Program, which is still up to this day. Everything just kept falling into place until I never heard back from Edward Hospital where I applied for a Patient Care Tech position. I didn't give up. I visited the Human Resources Department each week until I got that interview. After two months of relentlessly trying to get my foot in the door, I interviewed and got the job. I officially worked three 12-hour shifts a week on the med-surge floor.

I trained with many people that were surprised I had zero experience as a CNA and landed the position at the hospital while completing the courses to become a registered nurse. My plan of working three nights with 12-hour shifts was well on its way... until reality set in. I worked four nights as a PCT at the hospital and it was a killer. I give tremendous respect to all people in the medical field. In four nights, I helped with three dead bodies, and the exhaustion was UNREAL. FOUR nights, that is all it took. As I crawled into my car after finishing the hospital work shift, I called my husband. I felt like a complete failure and told him how it was NOT for me. I cried, knowing in my heart that this journey of becoming a nurse was not the path I was meant to go on. I felt like I had wasted my time, my family's time, not to mention our money that we desperately needed.

Why would I quit after all that time and effort? You might think that four days wouldn't give anyone enough time to make an educated decision, but I knew in my heart that it wasn't for me.

About two years after what felt like the most epic fail of my life, and six months after my Gran passed away, my Aunt (her sister that was 20 years younger) was diagnosed with stage four breast cancer and went into hospice care. If you have gone through devastating loss, you know the feeling of everything blurring before your eyes. Nothing is clear and life basically turns into a series of motions. And even though my Uncle had 24-hour caretakers in their home, my Aunt cried, telling me she didn't want strangers changing or bathing her.

I made the decision to stay with her each day for the last month of her life and take care of these needs, so she felt secure and comfortable. Each time I lifted her up our eyes would meet, tears started streaming down our faces while love was felt. I would not have been able to correctly care for her had I not earned my nursing assistant license. Between meeting Maddie, and the knowledge I put into practice taking care of my Aunt in her last days, a feeling of failure became a feeling of purpose.

PIVOT IS NOT A SWEAR WORD

You know that swear jar mom had when you were growing up? Yeah, well, before COVID-19, the word "pivot" was on the list. My strategy in business was to never describe my actions as "pivoting" through change. I chose the softer, gentler word, adjusting.

After the pandemic hit, a 180-degree pivot is the move everyone in the public service industry needed to make. Keep in mind, our ways of working may completely change, but if the reasons why we love what we do does not change, we will survive. When you LOVE what you do and the reasons why you do them, you will succeed. The scenery and horizon may look completely different, but the same focus and end goal results in success. Your reactions to the changes around us will be what catapults you to the next stage in life. For instance, COVID-19 is a chapter in your book of life, it does not define who you are. Your actions do.

OVERCOMING FEAR OF FUTURE UNCERTAINTY

I sat outside a store manager's office waiting for our touch base on business. I was very early and was just getting caught up on a few administrative tasks when she opened the door to the office.

"Oh, you are early, this actually works out...I have a busy afternoon." She shrugged, took a deep breath, and grimly motioned for me to come inside her office while grabbing a box of tissues. "You know, for later." she said.

I knew exactly what she needed it for. There are a couple times a year when everyone in a leadership role holds their breath as staffing updates are released. This year was one of the worst I have seen. She grabbed the tissue for when people find out they no longer have a position.

My heart sank and my stomach instantly felt nauseated. I knew this feeling all too well.

The year was 2018, the start of the recession.

After working in the Cosmetics Industry for 16 years, I was having a very successful run managing all the freelance makeup artists in Chicago. The position entailed scheduling, training, hiring, coaching, developing, and communicating with the executives. Nonetheless, things were getting moved around and there were changes afoot within the company. People were being let go. Scheduled "status" calls were popping up and everyone's phone was ringing.

Familiar with such scheduled calls, I was usually the person doing the calling about lack of hours, or even last minute elimination of shifts. What I learned is that even though a freelancer was hired knowing the possibility of such changes, those calls were never easy, and there was never a good time to make them.

My situation was much different than a freelancer. The position consisted of salary pay and benefits, averaging many, MANY more than 40 hours a week. The workload never bothered me because I LOVED my job. To be quite honest, I felt untouchable because of how much people relied on me! The money wasn't tremendous for the hours worked, but I was confident that the future was bright. *How could anyone even possibly THINK of eliminating my job- that would be stupid.*

I remember it like it was yesterday. On a Monday in March, a call popped up in my schedule for a "status" from a corporate leader for that Thursday. I was frantic, but not because of what you would think. Overwhelmed with organizing an annual meeting with all the artists on my team *on that Thursday* - I did NOT have time for this call! I quickly replied asking if we can reschedule for the day after my very important meeting. I asked my bosses boss to reschedule my call. After all, it was probably just going to be about how great my contributions are, right? Friday at 10 a.m. it was. Thursday was one of the best meetings I have ever conducted, and my team felt energized and excited about the mission of the program I developed. Suddenly I couldn't wait for "that call" to discuss how extraordinary it was and what the future will bring in my career!

Friday at 10 am the phone rang. Everything was organized with my planner, laptop, notepad, pen, and coffee. The first thing on the agenda was a big CONGRATULATIONS on a terrific meeting! It was the talk around town how impressive the day transpired! As a big smile beamed across my face, I heard, "Ok, now open up your laptop and proceed to your email. There is a letter of separation that was just sent, and we are not moving forward with your position." Sure enough, the letter of termination was right there. The severance package, everything, was right before my eyes.

Everything else was a bit blurry after that. I was told that I could continue my position, but the hours could fluctuate, and nothing was guaranteed. I was even told to be creative in naming my position and the flexibility could even work out for the best since I have young children at home. Despite the efforts and kind words, the result was still the same. I said," Thank you, but no thank you," fully aware that this job was unmistakably full-time and therefore... I was officially eliminated.

I lived and breathed for my company and my teams. It was a horrible time. I knew that I could get another job in the industry. I had the reputation. I had the experience. But it still felt like a thousand-pound elephant on my chest when I woke up every morning.

Unsure how to handle this tremendous amount of uncertainty and constant mind chatter, I started running. I am absolutely not a runner but needed SOMETHING to release this pent-up energy. Self-help podcasts were a staple in my digital library. I learned from people like Simon Sinek and Brendan Bouchard. Running to listen ended up being the objective and, in turn, there was an emotional release. A gratitude for life had taken over and from then on, a sense of presence in each moment. I finally learned to let go of trying to control tomorrow and just started living for the day. With every step on the pavement, I was becoming more self-aware. I was growing.

EMBRACING CHANGE

What is fear? Here's how the Merriam-Webster dictionary defines it: "An unpleasant, often strong emotion caused by anticipation of awareness of danger."
To me, fear is a loss of security. Fear distracts us from our goals and aspirations. When circumstances change it leads to unchartered territories; reaction towards the unexpected will determine fate. It is time to embrace any disruption that arrives and take it as an opportunity to open your eyes to bigger opportunities. The more you experience change, the more flexible and resilient you become. You can get through any situation and conquer any fear in front of you. You will be at the bottom and reach the top many times in your life, and you will persevere to find solutions. The

challenges you face are growing opportunities and will give you permission to take action and move forward. My four principles of change are:

1. Do not be too quick to react
2. Focus on what you are good at
3. Build knowledge and skill
4. Picture yourself where you want to be and act like you are already there

For a great skincare regime, you need the right products. It's no different in life. Armor up to change with these four fool-proof techniques.

1) The only thing you can control is your response to a situation. Give yourself at least 24 to 48 hours to grasp what is happening around you. Most situations are not life or death and waiting to respond will give a better perspective. Take the time to think about a circumstance and strategize your next action. I like to take the time to write down the situation with pros and cons while discussing with someone I trust. This thought process will give you a clearer perspective rather than a "knee jerk" reaction. A plan of action will almost always manage your fear and prepare you for success.

2) Focusing on your natural abilities will shift your mindset to one of positivity and optimism. What are some of your success stories that you take great pride in? What would your friends or co-workers say you are naturally good at? List them. Feel proud.

3) Learning equals personal growth. The more we learn the less we fear. Think of it like a puzzle. Each time you learn something, you create this link to learn something more. It builds this endless chain of knowledge to create a beautiful picture. Change is what allows us to learn new skills and become empowered to take action.

4) Elevate yourself rather than waiting for others to elevate you. Before I was a cosmetic executive, I subscribed to a cosmetic executive email list. I listened to beauty CEOs and networked with entrepreneurs in my free time. I wanted to discover insight as if I were already at that level, to see the bigger picture of the industry I wanted to grow in. If you are looking for professional growth, always look for more information than what is given to you, and gain the knowledge needed to get where you want to be.

I would not be writing this book if my position was not eliminated (thank you, Ms. Awesome Destiny!!). I took the time to understand what provided me the most meaning in life and take a journey of finding my true authenticity. I became an open book (no pun intended), and I am no longer timid about my opinions of how to better the industry. There is a certain type of empathy that grows inside when you deal with any kind of loss. Sales positions are a roller coaster. You could be the head of the pack one day, and the tail end of the race the next.

You may be reading this thinking how some of your stores have expanded and flourished and not even a global pandemic can change that. Some of you just read my story and your heart started beating because you know that feeling of uncertainty all too well. Either way, any position could get realigned or a company could restructure at any time. Flexibility and an open mind will help prepare and navigate actions to overcome these obstacles. Never slow down and let your reputation be your resume.

WITHOUT THE RAIN, THERE WOULD NEVER BE RAINBOWS

Three months after my position was eliminated, I accepted an executive position I have worked toward my entire life. Leading with authenticity and sincerity while helping others find their purpose became my sole focus to have the greatest #IMPACT.

Your purpose will replace work with passion. Take the time to invest in yourself, and soon you won't be wishing away the minutes. Appreciate every moment and its potential. This book is a tool to help you excel in the retail service industry, and realize that the meaning of service will fall under many new categories as we face unchartered territories. It is a business to meet and exceed your customers, the companies, and personal expectations. Fulfillment comes from personal connection, not by tasking or checking off a list.

Beginners: This is not an afterschool job where you can do your homework "when it's slow". We WORK. We do not stand around and chat with our arms crossed waiting for customers to approach us. Make sure you have sustainable energy, thick skin, positive attitude, entrepreneurial spirit, and a true passion for sales, service, and beauty. We count on you to connect with new customers and have a new perspective that we can learn from. We need your fresh perspective, fearlessness, and fiery passion. We need you.

Seasoned: Don't wait until your position is in jeopardy to be re-engaged with your job. Honestly, it may be too late by then. You have been in this industry long enough to know it is not the same as 20 years ago. I smile every time I remember the red rope "stanchions" to keep everyone in line as they waited to be serviced. If you go back even further, customers had to take a number like at the deli because they needed US, not the other way around. If you haven't already, it is time for you to modernize and be open to new ideas, tools, and ways to service the clients. You add value to this industry when you realize the value you must give. Your experience, adaptability, and activation through change is needed now more than ever.

Leaders: Customer-facing employees are the secret to your success. It is your job to keep the train moving, to inspire, to teach, and to show your teams that you wake up every morning for THEM. Your success is measured by the worst person on your team, and keep in mind that if everyone was as skilled as you, they would have your job. It is your responsibility to keep your teams educated, feeling safe, productive, and engaged. Consumers, shoppers, customers, clients, etc... are the reason we are in business. If we didn't ring the register, the doors would close, absolutely. Keep in mind that the people working and servicing those customers are the most important part of your business. When cutting budgets or corners, the investment of your employees should never be included on that list. The quality of leadership is more important than ever, and as much as you are obsessed with your customer, be as obsessed with who is servicing them. There is no other choice but to be open to new ideas and recognize people on your team for trying new things. Innovators are what is needed through such drastic changes; therefore need leaders to support and help execute.

THE AMAZON EFFECT

First, let me be clear that I am a BIG fan of online shopping. An Amazon package is delivered to the Feeley household almost every day of the week and a savior throughout the pandemic. We order bed sheets to batteries--and I feel grateful for the ease of convenience it offers. E-Commerce is a very important part of our retail success and in some cases may even entice consumers to step foot into a store.

BOPIS (Buy Online and Pick Up In-Store) is another example of consumer behavior that you might think marginalizes what we at the beauty counter do, but that is completely, unequivocally incorrect. What matters are the actions we take while customers step through the door. As stores reopen and rebuild, every single customer is a gift and should be communicated with care and sincerity. Digital experiences help us to learn quicker, communicate faster, and share anything to the world with a click of a button. The most important question I have is…. *What are YOU able to offer that online does not?*

Even before the COVID-19 pandemic, I remember one of my co-workers, let's call her Rita Realist, expressed how frustrated she was about the "online specials only" and she felt there was no way to compete in the store. I asked her, "What do you think you could offer the customers that online cannot?"

Rita replied, "I cannot compete with online. They have discounts and free samples that I am not given. Just today, I helped a woman for almost an hour recommending the correct products for her. When I asked her what she would like to take home, she asked me to write the items down so she could order it online and take advantage of the deals. I have just about had enough. Do you want to know what I did?"

"Eeeeeks that is tough. What did you do?" I asked
Rita's eyebrows lifted and said, "I wrote down all the wrong products and sent her on her way."

Rita, I know you are reading this and thinking to yourself, "Yep, I sure did. That ignorant, selfish woman wasted my time and how does anyone expect me to achieve my goals when I am set up to fail?"

I know Rita is not alone in thinking this way. Yes, online will have different promotions that may not be in store at that time. But what online does not have, is YOU. Rita wrote down the wrong products out of frustrated emotion. The customer will probably purchase those incorrect products and will not return as a customer again (let alone visit Rita Realist again). This was a no-win solution. Here is the thing. You are not going to stop customers from purchasing online. It is their choice to do so. The situation could have been handled differently, and like a domino effect, lead to a totally different outcome. Because the truth is that you have the power, the presence, and the human-centered love, to give customers every reason to buy from YOU. Let me give you an example.

Rita could have written down the correct items and supported her customer taking advantage of online specials. Rita already had a connection with her to follow up on her products and continue to build a relationship. Keep in mind, you don't have to go to bed on the first date. It is ok to build a relationship based on integrity and trust. Rita would have built her reputation as a trusted advisor and friend so the customer would most likely return, especially after Rita took the time to service her. Then, the customer could refer Rita to her friends or family.

If you do right by the customer and company you work for, it will always come back one way or another. Never give up because hard work always pays off. I am a true believer that what you give is what you get. This is a lesson that would change Rita Realist's life and it can change yours too.

WHERE IT ALL BEGAN

In 1998 I walked into a retailer feeling horrible about myself. At 18, I had such bad acne that my face actually HURT. I felt like I had so much to say but zero confidence to say it.

I wanted to completely hide away, and I went looking for ways to also hide my face. I grabbed my money that I made from my part-time position at Abercrombie and Fitch and set out for a quick skin fix.

I stepped into a large department store at the time and walked straight to cosmetics. Before I entered, I took a great big breath hoping no one would talk to me as I was embarrassed of how I looked. A smiling woman approached me and quickly found out I was shopping for foundation. She asked me questions and told me that she would not only find the best foundation for my skin, but also the best complexion products to help. This beauty advisor offered me a seat, walked through my new skincare regimen, and detailed the direction of how to apply the new products that suddenly gave me renewed hope.

Well over my budget, I purchased what was suggested. She sampled me on the product I wasn't ready to take home that day, with instructions on how to use it while gathering my information to follow up. It wasn't too long after that I realized she literally changed my life!

My skin improved drastically, and I had my confidence back. I am forever grateful to her for taking the time to gain my trust so she could have a candid and vulnerable conversation about my skin (A VERY BIG DEAL), recommending the best products, and following up to see how I was doing.

Thank you, mystery women, for not only saving my skin, but introducing me to what true service is all about! You could have just gotten an effortless foundation sale, but instead you changed my life forever. *I am grateful that I had to go to the store rather than clicking a button to purchase my item. If you are helping someone virtually or in person, connect on a deeper level to find out about how the person is feeling and the reasons behind the shopping. You will gain a friend, not just a customer. A click alone can never be a confidante to a customer. You can.*

Trust your instincts and have faith that things are always meant to be. Then take that confidence and passion and share it with the world.

5

ACTIVATE

—

Yes, it's about more than the lipstick. Now, you have started on the journey of self-discovery, but actions are what tell the full story. The extra steps you take are what will set you apart from mediocrity. The extra effort is what will make your light shine brighter than the rest. The extra time and investment you give yourself and to others is what provides fulfillment. You are not in this alone and the second half of this book will provide a roadmap to help guide you in the right direction. Your eyes on this page tell me you're hungry to redefine your success. We start with the interview.

THE INTERVIEW

Leaders: In interviews, the candidate should be doing most of the talking. I like to call this the 80-20 method. The candidate should be doing 80 percent of the talking and you should be the

20 percent. It is easy to talk about specifics, especially if you are getting a good vibe, but now is not the time. Base your questions around the needs of the business as well as the team. Ask for specific examples or for them to expand on their thoughts. If you have any 'constructive' feedback that would be encouraging and helpful in the future, don't hold back. You have so much to offer, and take that opportunity to share expectations, even when not moving forward with the candidate. Don't think of it as a waste of your time, rather an investment in people, and it will contribute to your reputation.

One day I had an interview set up at a retailer for a freelance position at 10am. I was meeting the candidate, Carla Candid, at the cosmetic counter. When I arrived, I glanced around for the candidate. The only person I saw (besides my team working) was a customer. One of my artists quickly pulled me aside and told me that the person who I thought was a customer, was the interviewee.

Sure enough, the "customer" was indeed Carla Candid. Carla was a naturally beautiful, statuesque woman dressed in dark denim jeans, a holiday sweater, UGG boots, and not a stitch of makeup. I told my team I would be back shortly, and they just gave me a half smile and quiet nod with their eyebrows up.

Carla and I slipped away to a secluded area and I had a feeling that this would be quick. Carla had plenty of experience from years ago, before she had children, and proceeded to tell me about her passion for the beauty industry. She also told me that she came straight from the gym and apologized for not "looking her best." I briefly thought about asking Carla the standard interviewing questions, but I knew my decision was to not move forward.

In the moment, I decided not to fill the air with words but to just be honest. "Carla, it sounds to me that you have incredible experience and you are extremely engaging."

Carla nodded in agreement.

I asked her, "My first impression is not matching the story of passion and skill that you have for makeup, since you are not wearing any. I am curious to know why?"

Carla apologized, and told me she always has makeup on but that day she didn't. I thought we were on the way to wrap up the interview, and then she started tearing up. Carla proceeded to tell me that she had been out of the job market and beauty industry for many years due to an abusive relationship. She told me she was going through a very difficult divorce and wants to keep her children safe, secure, and supported. My heart grew instantly because of her bravery in life, and the courage she showed to open up. Carla concluded her story by explaining the uncertainty she felt of even working at the moment due to these circumstances.

I thanked Carla Candid for confiding in me and appreciated

her honesty.

"I have a plan," I announced. I wanted Carla to take the time she needed to figure out what was best for her and her family. When she was truly ready to reach out to me, we would schedule a follow up interview. I gave her the things I will need from her to be prepared, and would give this advice to everyone:

- A hard copy of your resume (even if the interviewer has a digital one)
- Makeup brushes for application- and be ready to apply makeup (you do not need to know product information by heart, but it shows the comfortability with social acumen, touch, and application)
- Applicable and/or relevant social media or website account, prepared to show
- Have pictures of makeup application you have done readily available
- Dress in all professional black (nothing sleeveless, no leggings)
- Wear your makeup as you would wear it to work
- Availability of your schedule
- Any questions you may have about the position and benefits
- If interviewing for a brand, be ready to talk about the products and what you love about them.

A month later Carla Candid called me and inquired about a position. I kept my word and met with her. She had taken the advice I gave her. She was prepared, looked the part, and executed the "role-play, hands-on" portion of the interview flawlessly. I'm proud to say Carla Candid became Carla Can-Do. She has had a very successful career and is one of the most sought-after make-up artists in the industry.

Beginners and Seasoned: Do your research about any company you are interviewing with. Be well informed and come prepared knowing about the company's history and specific products.

Leaders: People work for people. Always remember that.

6

THE CONTROLLABLES: FROM HIRING TO HYGIENE

Never settle. If you wouldn't put a product on yourself, don't put it on someone else. Hygiene is a priority for your own safety and for the safety of your customers. There are certain things you cannot control: traffic, trends, or the economy. BUT, the things you CAN control are presentation and representation. Always look your best and tell a story with your merchandise and products.

HYGIENE EQUALS HEALTH

When disruption hits, it could be a deliberate warning to prevent something even worse. Hygiene equals health. It is our duty to make sure we are doing everything in our power to protect ourselves and our customers. Stay up to date and informed with current recommendations from your National Disease Control. Do not cut corners, go the extra mile and be on high alert. Hygiene and health recommendations have ZERO wiggle room and no exceptions. Speak up to your leadership about any ideas or practices that can improve health and safety because your input is invaluable.

WHEN HIRING, DON'T SETTLE

To my beauty bosses:

When hiring for your team, a very important lesson I learned was settling to fill "the job". When a position is open and worry about coverage affecting sales is top of mind, the temptation to "just fill the position" can be overwhelming. Many of us have been there and learned our lesson, but if you have yet to, this time will come, I guarantee it. For those that have already learned the lesson of settling to fill, the future temptation never goes away.

Now it is time to really think about the consequences when we settle.

Seasoned Sally applied for a counter manager position that had been open for three months. Three months of no "official leader", no strategist of the business, no consistent motivator, and let's not forget, short in staff. The retailer reached out so I could interview her, and I was quite thrilled about the possibility of finally filling this position. Sally's resume was ON POINT, with over two decades of management experience and growth sales results.

She has worked for a few retailers and she was very well versed on how to drive business.

Sally met me in a store, and EVERYONE knew her, hugging her and so happy to be running into one another. It was almost like this woman was the mayor of the cosmetic department! I started to question, why didn't I know her?

The interview was seamless until I asked Sally why she was interested in this particular retailer. She told me she loved the fact that reviews are not only determined on sales, but other aspects of the job. When probing a bit more, Seasoned Sally told me the real reason why she left her last position. It was because the sales expectations were incredibly difficult, and even though Sally still made it happen, she didn't enjoy personal pressure.

I felt a tiny little knot in my stomach. Uh oh. (Devil on shoulder) She isn't crazy about sales goals.

(Angel). BUT this is a different brand. She will not feel pressure because we believe in our products. Besides, she has a strong team that will support her.

(Devil) It won't be easier. It will be the same. It is the same responsibilities and the only difference is the name on the building. I need someone to be HUNGRY, driven, and motivate the team to do the same!

(Angel) Her experience speaks for itself. We need to fill this job and she could probably do it with her eyes closed.

I wrapped up the interview feeling a bit torn. My next step was to ask our mutual connections as references. *C'mon people, please give me a rave review, I need to fill this job!*

The reviews were mostly positive. Nothing "terrible" and I had one FANTASTIC reference which made me seal the deal. Seasoned Sally was hired!!!!

Here is the thing. When you hire someone that you are not one hundred percent positive that they will be the right fit, or maybe not yet ready, then don't do it. FIT is everything, and you are hiring PEOPLE. When you hire PEOPLE for your own agenda, it just isn't the right thing to do. You could be unintentionally setting them up to fail, or even act as a "bandage" due to timing.

What I should have done was speak to Seasoned Sally one more time to explain the commitments. I should have asked HER OPINION of specific potential circumstances, what actions she would take, and HOW SHE WOULD FEEL. If I did that, maybe we could have had an honest conversation about what Sally's motivations are and what really gets her up out of bed in the morning. Her talent could have been shifted in the right direction, in a role that was a great fit FOR HER.

Sally did not stay in the counter manager position for a day over four months. She left for the same reason it didn't work out in her last position, and to be honest, and as my kids would say, it ended "kinda sucky."

About a month after Sally's departure, a position opened at a different retailer as a full-time beauty advisor. After reaching out to her and having an honest conversation of where her passion lives, she is now doing what she loves the most AND where she thrives. Sally doesn't have to worry about anything but making connections with her customers and building her own business through relationships. She is happy, and I know in my heart that Sally will stay there for a long time because it is the right fit.

THE BIG PICTURE

I could have saved time and stress with this amazing employee (in a different role), if I had just taken the time to look past my agenda and desperation to fill a position.

Confidence in hiring the right people for the right job, is not only a gift you are giving yourself and your company, but it is a gift for the person. That initial honesty and transparency will heighten the success rate of the candidate and may be a learning for you as well. When you have that voice on your shoulder or that little knot in your stomach that is (even a bit) nervous, my advice is to take their life as seriously as yours. Gambling on the chance it may or may not work out is not fair to the person you are hiring and it is a top priority to put their best interests before your own.

What can you control? No matter what your position in

retail--whether you are a manager or associate--the answer is, you control a lot of things beyond the obvious.

SIX DEGREES OF COSMETICS.

The world is small, and the cosmetic industry world is even smaller. This chapter applies to everyone at any level. From Beauty Advisor to Executive level leadership, word gets around if you apply at a different company. Trust and transparency is the number one rule when it comes to your reputation in your career. Best practice is to always be open and honest with your employer or even a potential employer.

I know what you are thinking. Everyone knows anyone that knows someone in this industry. It is like this circle of friends even if you have not yet met. It is not a secret if you apply at numerous companies, or sometimes even just converse with other people about the possibility. The walls have ears in every aspect of the sense. I am not being overly dramatic or exaggerating. My first piece of advice is, DO NOT apply at several places because we get calls about each and every one of them. My second piece of advice is, beware of what you say to your peers and what you post on social media. Even if you post the tiniest negative blurb for a minute on social media, you can safely assume someone will remember it forever. ALWAYS stay professional.

Typically, when a job seeker applies for a position for a cosmetic brand inside a retailer, protocol is interviewing with both retailer and brand, then the decision is agreed upon whether to move forward or not. Communication between the two are very open, honest, and forthright.

Everyone in the cosmetic industry is connected in some way, shape, or form. Be honest and speak up with people as opportunities or challenges may arise. If you feel nervous for any reason, find a mentor that you can trust. I always tell people they can confidentially reach out to me anytime for my opinion and guidance (you too, just DM me on Instagram). As a leader, set people up for success and happiness. As an associate, be honest and transparent. As a result, everyone wins.

LEADERS BUILD THE SUCCESS ROADMAP

Transparency holds true. To my FELLOW LEADERS: WE ARE ALL IN THIS TOGETHER and when we deliberately work together, success is imminent. Do not hold people back from growing because you want to keep them stagnant for self-serving reasons. Equally, do not recommend someone unless they truly have your endorsement.

The purpose of leadership is to help people reach their goals and platform them for success. If you are unsure of what to do in any given situation, just do the right thing for everyone involved. When decisions for people's lives are based on personal success and not the success of others, it's time for an ethics check.

Believe me, it all comes back around, and your reputation is at stake. Is the grass greener on the other side for you? For the person standing next to you? Probably not. The grass under your feet, though, has the potential for being the most lush and vibrant of all.

7

SALES GOALS AND MAKING MONEY

—

Knowing your expectations in order to achieve them is the key factor to success in your career with a company. Every large or small goal that is achieved builds on top of one another, creating a sturdy foundation for growth. It is imperative to not only participate, but to fully engage with the vision of success and celebrate even the smallest of feats. This chapter is about getting down and dirty with what some people may find uncomfortable, and that is the money part. We must be honest that at the end of the day, we are working for a "profit" and this is what keeps the doors open. When the doors stay open, we can continue to impact lives and give the gift of beauty to the world. I will also highlight selling tips that will focus your efforts on positively impacting your customers, while ringing the register without the guilt of "selling."

SELLING IS SERVICE

There are many occupations and titles that are in the cosmetic retail world, and in this book, we concentrate on the positions that are consumer-facing. The descriptions may be different in every retailer or brand, and structure of a company can vary. One thing that is an absolute common theme in all "beauty boss" positions, is the intention of producing sales while giving a customized service, whether you are directly or indirectly ringing the register.

Different goals are presented when you are hired, and we will touch on important questions to ask when you start a new job. The most common positions in the cosmetic retail environment are (and not limited to):

Beauty advisor: Offers personalized service and experience to clients while maintaining sales goals.

Counter manager: Responsible for the development of beauty advisors on their team, overall customer service, merchandising, education of products, productivity, and sales goals.

Cosmetic department manager: Retail supervisors that manage employees while responsible for overall department sales goals.

Freelance makeup artist: Specifically, a contracted employee for a brand or company. An "on-call" make-up artist/specialist with typically no benefits offered and inconsistent schedule.

These definitions are extremely general and not official job descriptions. They are a basic overview and depending on the retailer, may have several more titles and responsibilities.

Please take note that in any position, your managers work for YOU. They make sure you have the optimal environment to allow you to give exceptional service to your customers and sell the products. They appreciate your hard work, transparency/honesty, and your ability to problem solve. Stay positive, and if you do have a complaint, offer a solution.

Leaders: The dynamic of "trickle down" politics is a thing of the past. Trickle up is how you will gain insight and learn how to effectively grow your business. Leading a productive, positive, engaged, and well-informed team is a necessity, but you will learn more about your business from the people in front of your customers. Ask your employees questions to gain insight on what works, what opportunities/challenges they are facing, and any suggestions for improvement.

STORE MANAGEMENT DEMANDS CURIOSITY

I have been on both sides of the coin. Cosmetic beauty sales associates have two types of support if they work for a specific brand and store (retailer that issues the paychecks). As retail evolves, management positions are getting more layers of responsibility on their plate, and sometimes it is like a race against time trying to get tasks checked off. Retailers rely on the vendors to inspire and motivate, and vendors rely on retailers to check in and help hold the team accountable. Daily recognition, training, and education is an integral part of a store management job. Always remember you are in your position for a reason, and people on your team want to learn from you. Create a legacy and conquer the impact on your team.

Leaders: All too often the administrative part of your position can get in the way of observing and providing feedback on the sales floor. There is nothing worse than a manager that is in the office for the majority of the time. Find a way to prioritize your admin time and commit to side by side floor presence with your team. When traffic is busy, it is easy to automatically be on the sales floor to offer an extra hand, but what can you do to elevate your team on lower traffic days?

It is ok if you don't know where to start. ASK your team. You will find that they will be honest in what they want to learn, therefore will help productivity and service when you are not around. Your employees will appreciate the time you give and respect the leadership and direction. The associates will be more open to feedback if they feel that you are able to walk in their shoes. This is called leading by example. How could you ask someone to do something if you have not done it yourself? Get out of your office, buckle up, drink some coffee, and get ready to be uncomfortable. Every day I challenge you for 20 minutes (any random time) to stand back and observe your department or store and truly look at the engagement with customers. What is working? Is everyone engaged and ready to service? How does your department or store look, inviting or unorganized? If it looks unkempt, it does not look clean. If it does not look clean, then it looks unsafe. If it is unsafe, then online only here we come.

Beginners AND Seasoned: Train your trainer. Meaning, no one will know what you need help with unless you ask. If you do not speak up on something that you are struggling with, everyone will assume you have a grasp on it. My mentor taught me this concept on my first day. Do not let your pride get in your way of asking for help or admitting you do not know something. Acting like you know everything will only stunt your growth. Your job is to be honest, curious, and ask questions.

Leaders (again): If someone on your team is asking for help in a specific way, listen carefully to what they are needing. It takes courage and vulnerability to raise a hand and admit needing help or assistance. It could actually be scary because no one likes to be perceived as inadequate or incapable. Respect the vulnerability as you respond to questions and try to be empathetic and understanding. Empowering your employees to try to figure it out and then providing feedback is an approach, as some learn by action first. Others are visual learners, like myself, and learn by observation, then action. It is important to understand how each person on your team learns for you to adjust teaching methods accordingly.

TEACHING: You are teachers. You are in your position due to knowing that it is your job to elevate others.

Every day be curious. Ask yourself these questions:

- What did I teach/train someone on my team about today?
- What did I observe about my team as an opportunity for the business?
- When teaching/training, was it interactive? Were you talking at them or working together using actionable and hands-on experience?
- Did you give a measurable goal to your team member(s) to ensure activation of this new skill?
- What is your plan for following up on the teaching/training measurable goal?
- Follow up is one of the most important aspects of training. It provides a discipline to activate the new skill learned and accountability. Follow up on the follow through.

EVERYONE DESERVES OPPORTUNITY

At one time in my career I managed freelance makeup artists, and I hired one of my best friends, Layla, as a makeup artist and skin specialist. I met her when I was younger, at nursing school, and both having a passion for beauty, we became instant friends. As time went by, Layla grew into my other half, one of those friends that you could always count on and trust. We had a lot in common, and work ethic was one of them. It was a no-brainer to have her join my team. Layla was a licensed cosmetologist with most experience with hair, and makeup was a bit foreign to her. I reassured her that I would make sure she was well trained and ready to succeed. I spent two full days with her, side-by-side training her.

The first day we role-played. She was the customer and I was servicing her, giving her the full experience of what was expected. Layla then reversed and practiced on me. I am a true believer that learning happens when we see, touch, and feel. The second day was the action. Layla serviced clients and I observed, helped when needed, and gave feedback. I continued to invest in her education and growth and made it a priority she succeeded. She caught on after that, and ended being one of the top salespeople on the team.

Not too long after, I had an employee that had been

consistently underperforming. I tried to give her tips and tricks on how to close the sale, observed, and gave feedback. I thought there was just no hope, it just wasn't a good fit. Layla was very observant and pulled me aside.

"Did you give her the same chance you gave me? Did you train her?" Layla asked.

"I'm not sure I understand this question. Of course I trained her." I was a bit frustrated she even asked me.

"No, did you train her like you trained me," she pushed me.

OUCH. I didn't. Not saying that I did not give her training, just not as intense as Layla. She knew it, and that is why she asked me. I appreciated that more than she could ever know, because it changed my lens on the development of time vested in each person. My pride was a bit bruised that Layla questioned that, but I was forever grateful.

CREATE YOUR OWN PATH AND DO NOT FOLLOW OTHERS

For the most part, people are great coming out of the gate. When a new job or position starts, their momentum is fierce and energy is heightened. It will feel like all of a sudden, but over a period of time, the momentum is lost. It feels acceptable to perhaps "hang out" with your co-workers, or even spend more time on your phone (not working). You may not even realize this is happening but there are "cues" that I want to make you aware of.

When you are unmotivated you feel excessively tired. Time starts dragging by and you cannot wait for the workday to be over, therefore the continuous glances at your watch or phone. You get easily distracted and you do not follow through on tasks or responsibilities you may have. Productivity suffers. Maybe you feel defeated. The effort you have put forth in the past has not been as rewarding as you envisioned, or you feel like you are the only one that is working hard, and it just isn't fair. Usually this happens for two reasons.

First, your co-workers may be less motivated than you. It happens. They may not mind mediocrity, and do only what is expected. It is very easy to follow that lead and not make your own path. It is ok that you don't just want to get by, but you have this urge to go after business and go the extra mile when it comes to service. You must be strong and resist the urge to fall into the "make the donuts" trap. To my youthful readers you may have to look that up, just google Dunkin Donuts commercials in the 80's. You start going through the motions in an industry that is anything but predictable.

KNOW THE EXPECTATIONS

Your job expectations are directly tied to your company. A Profit and Loss (P&L) statement within a company reveals their net income after expenses, which helps in the decision-making process. It is important to know that employees are an investment, and companies expect a return on that investment (ROI). Positions are usually based on sales or how the position #IMPACTS sales and, therefore, profit.

When accepting a job, make sure you ask for the company's business goals, the team goals, and the official job description. You cannot achieve a goal- unless you know the goal to achieve.

Leaders: Cosmetic leader, Jill Foerster, gives this advice. "Give the goals and expectations before they are hired on the team." She explains that when candidates accept a position, they are signing up for a certain dollar amount to sell for the year. This is the participation that is needed to contribute to the total sales goal. If for some reason an associate is short of their personal goal, then someone else not only has to achieve their sales, but also the shortage. If the person you hired does not have a measurable sales goal, communicate expectations on how their responsibilities ultimately affect the sales and success of the business. It is important for everyone that is hired to understand why their position exists, and how incredibly beneficial they are as a contributor.

15 specific questions to ask (take note!) before you start are:

1. What is the dress code?
2. What are the peak times of business?
3. Who is my direct report?
4. What does on-boarding look like?
5. How am I trained on the products?
6. What kind of events take place throughout the year? What are my expectations at these events?
7. How is the store performing/trending in sales for the year? Department? Cosmetic line? What is currently most challenging?
8. What are the rules of social media?
9. What is the customer follow up protocol and expectation?
10. Are there any loyalty programs available to the customers? Credit and Non-credit rewards?
11. What am I reviewed on? Is there a way to have a copy of a blank review?
12. What are my individual/counter sales goals for each WEEK, MONTH, and YEAR?
13. How do I keep track of my sales?
14. What should I expect my schedule to look like?
15. What is the growth potential within this organization? What is the hierarchy of positions?

10 questions for Seasoned and Leaders for self-assessment:

1. What were your top three accomplishments last year? What was the journey of how you got there?

2. What was your biggest failure last year and what did you learn from it?

3. How would you review yourself (circle one): growing, sustaining, or declining business? Give specific examples with results.

4. What were the controllables of your business for the past season? Uncontrollables? How did you navigate and offer solutions to the uncontrollables?

5. How did you impact sales and what was your measurable (i.e. sales volume)

6. What personal goal outside of work did you accomplish this past year?

7. What is a personal goal outside of work for the upcoming year?

8. What relationships are you most proud of in your place of work?

9. What relationships could you improve upon? What are some ideas to activate?

10. Why do you love what you do and how do you incorporate that each day?

10 questions for Leadership assessment:

1. How would you rate your team, from 1-5?
2. Define goals for your business and everyone on your team. What are their aspirations and how will you help them get there? What is your timeline?
3. What have you done to develop your team on a daily basis?
4. How have you made the work environment fun, interactive, and inclusive? Give specific examples with results.
5. Have you coached by telling, showing, or observing? Circle and give specific examples.
6. Have you treated each team member equally?
7. Do you see challenges for the upcoming year as exhausting or exhilarating? Remember energy breeds energy and be honest.
8. How have you recognized top performers and key players on your team? Has anyone been promoted in the last year?
9. If anyone left, list the reasons why.
10. What are some new innovative ideas to generate new business and awareness?

YOU ARE IN CHARGE OF YOUR BUSINESS

Beginners and Seasoned: Even as a beauty advisor, your individual business is your responsibility and it is imperative to know where your performance is at all times. One key fact is that you cannot own your business if you do not believe in what you are selling. Why sell products you believe in? Because you can't give value if you don't believe in what you are delivering. The whole purpose of selling is believing you will help the customer and business by what you are offering.

Just because you may work for a particular brand, does not mean that you are going to fall in love with all the products. Usually, it is because it may not be a direct benefit, therefore difficult to suggest or show it to customers. How can you sell or suggest something you don't love, but are confident it could still benefit other people? Also, if you work for a particular brand, you owe it to your customers to be well versed on other products to give an honest opinion. You should work for a company because you truly believe in their products/services, but that is not to say you can't suggest other products from different companies. This is how you build trust. It is as simple as being honest.

You are in charge of your business--all of it. This means connecting products you may not personally use, but still suggest to customers who could benefit from them. It is easy to sell what you love. You know how to apply the products and special tricks/ hacks to incorporate in your routine. People fall in love with what you are suggesting due to your passion and confidence. But what happens when a product isn't particularly right for you personally as the expert? Confidence drops, your voice sounds a bit robotic, and excitement vanishes.

You are not every customer though, and you owe it to them to do your research. Just because a product isn't necessarily right for you, does not mean that you will not have a customer need for it. Ask other co-workers their thoughts, and when possible, sample products to specific customers that could benefit from the features. Get multiple opinions, ask many questions, and voila.

Now you can understand why people would love the product, how it makes them feel, and the results they notice with their skin.

Specific examples of testimonials with truthful expectations customers can expect to receive is the way to go. When you do your research for the benefit of your customers, the excitement heightens, and that is when you make a difference in people's lives. My challenge to you is if you do not necessarily care for a product, do your research and understand why some people may just love it for themselves.

Leaders: You should not have to talk an employee into loving a product line that their job is to sell. If they don't love it, then they won't believe in it, and you do not want anyone selling just for a paycheck. They should suggest products for the benefit of the customer, not just a goal on a paper or money in their pocket. If either is the case, it is not a good fit and unfair to the customer.

HOW TO SELL ANYTHING TO ANYONE (AND FEEL REALLY GOOD ABOUT IT)

There are hundreds of "how to sell" books out there. These are my top 10 selling tips:

1) Sell products that you believe in. Have confidence in the advice you are giving to a customer. You are being truthful and helpful to your customers rather than trying to convince people to believe you. This is your character, values, and ethics all rolled into one. When you believe in your product/service, the passion is what fuels the success.

2) Don't assume that people know what you know. We are experts. Do not take for granted your knowledge of the littlest things. A simple application tip can be a life changer for someone.

3) Be a teacher. Your job is to make sure that your client can build the skills to confidently use the products they are purchasing. A common comment you will hear from your customers/clients is: "I wish I can bring you home with me" or "Could you come over to my house every morning?" I always tell them, "As long as you have coffee for me!" We laugh but then I always follow up with, "Don't worry it's not brain surgery! I will make sure you feel confident applying whatever you bring home today." You want to empower people to be their own expert.

4) When you do not offer your products or service, you

are making the decision for them. If you are not vocal about the amazing products that will have a positive impact on a person's life, then how will they choose whether to take advantage of them? People do not even get the chance to refuse or accept when zero effort is made, and that isn't fair.

5) *Do not assume what people want to spend, or not spend, their money on.* Do not be afraid to show a product because of its price tag. It could actually be offensive to not offer specific products because you are assuming it is "too expensive" for them.

6) *Remember ONE personal fact about your customer.* Remember by writing it down, then bring it up when you follow up with them. For instance, ask about the wedding they attended or about their grandchildren. It shows that you are listening and care about them as people, not just a sale.

7) *Be a directive seller and give a reason why.* You are an expert. In your opinion, tell them what they need in a very direct but sensitive way. People want to be told what they need, and they want you to feel confident in your recommendations.

8) *Know your products features vs. benefits.* A feature of something is what a product has. A benefit is what the product will do. Customers care most about the benefits so know the difference. Let the customers know why the product is a match for what they need and want first, then explain any bonus features/ benefits.

9) *Create a sense of urgency.* Why does someone need to purchase their products today? It could even just be how much they will love it and why.

10) *Always be honest and realize a positive attitude could change anyone's day.* Be the person who makes a difference in other people's lives. Did you know, even under a mask or on the phone, that a smile is contagious?

The trinity of personal, career, and company goals should all synchronize with one other in order to achieve success. When there is full understanding and awareness of each of them, the puzzle starts to fill in and the journey of expanding and redefining success begins to unveil.

8

WINNER IN THE DARK

—

You are amazing. Let me just say out of the box that there is nothing you can't do. You are a courageous, determined, beautiful BEAUTY BOSS. What makes you different from any top performing salesperson or executive? Absolutely nothing. You have two hands just like they do, and those top dogs put on pants one leg at a time, just like everyone else. Welcome. This chapter is just for you.

THE "LIGHTS" DON'T ALWAYS HAVE TO BE ON

"Win in the Dark" is a motto I learned from a high school football coach, Enrique Ibarra. I was volunteering at a local expo for my children's football and cheerleading organization with Enrique, when a student came up and said, "Hey, Coach!" and put out his hand to shake with Ibarra.

I observed as the conversation grew into a "laid back" excitement between coach and player. The eagerness for the upcoming season filled the air with energy and anticipation. When the student player went on his way, Enrique explained to me why he loves coaching. "In this particular case, this student was having serious behavioral issues at school and was on the fast track of the wrong path. He needed a role model and someone he could count on. I took on that role."

He continued to tell me how he implements the "win in the dark" strategy with his players. He explains to them that their integrity and efforts should always stay consistent, even when they think no one is looking.

Even if it may seem too dark to see, someone out there is always watching and noticing your actions. Stay true to yourself and always try your very best because it will always pay off.

THE TIME IS NOW

This is your time to build your clientele, your repeat business, and your reputation. Also, it is rewarding to make connections and teach your knowledge/skills to customers. Customers don't flock to cosmetic counters like they used to. And if you are in an environment that they are flocking into your store, more power to you, but do not celebrate until they COME BACK. It requires extreme effort to offer our services and make connections. If you do not offer your service, product, or an invitation to an event, then YOU are making the decision for the consumer. They do not even have a choice. That is so sad when that happens, and it is not fair to the customer.

Beginners: As a new beauty advisor, your day looks much different than a seasoned beauty advisor. For instance, Natalie Newbie and Veteran Vanessa are both full-time and work for the same brand. Even though Natalie is new, and Vanessa has been there for years, the sales goals are still the exact same because they are distributed by the hours worked. The path to get to the same goal will look much different.

Vanessa's large part of customer service is contacting her customers over the phone, email, or text. She follows up with them and informs them of either new products, events, or promotions. Natalie Newbie will not be able to spend time following up because she is just starting to build a clientele. Natalie will be productive by approaching new customers and offering services for most of her time.

As someone new, make your own path. You cannot compare what your day looks like and stay motivated with your extra effort of putting yourself out there. You will have to get creative as "services" will shift as time passes. Start thinking of ways to create awareness of what you have to offer. Introduce yourself to EVERYONE that works with you. If you are unsure what to do, then you MUST ask a valuable resource to get direction. Never stand and do nothing. Do something productive that gives you real results in your job performance. There is a difference between looking busy and being productive. Looking busy serves no purpose and there is no time to waste.

ALL LEVELS OF LEARNING:
PRACTICE, PRACTICE, PRACTICE.

I used to HATE ROLE PLAYING. I am not exaggerating. "Despise" is actually the word that comes to mind. When I am put on the spot, and have to "act" out a situation, I get awkward and trip over my words. I think my tongue deforms as my body rejects it. My selling and interpersonal skills instantly go right down the drain. Sounds so pleasant, right?

Until I realized WHY role playing is so important. Take the pressure off yourself. Role playing is for practice, whether you are learning how to offer or explain a new product, use a certain technique, or demonstrate a new service. If you were already perfect at it, you wouldn't be role playing! And if you have perfected it, then help someone that hasn't yet. My trick is practicing until you have it down perfectly. This allows you to feel comfortable and consistent, but also able to incorporate the specific information or technique in different situations and circumstances. When we practice, we do the opposite of becoming a robot, we actually sound more like ourselves as we incorporate the influx of our voice and personality. That initial tongue deformation you may feel (like me) is the process of learning. You have no reason to ever feel embarrassed of learning. You should feel proud.

LEADERS: WHAT IS IN IT FOR ME?

A business manager pulled me aside one day and asked me for advice. "How should I keep motivated when my coworkers are asking me why I work so hard? It is discouraging when I see everyone relaxing around me and I am running circles around them trying to get everything done." He raised his eyebrows and asked, "What's the point?"

I looked at him, realizing how brave he was for being honest and forthright. There was confusion in his eyes with a look of despair begging to help make sense of his efforts. I asked him to compare his business with the peers questioning his overzealous work ethic. I asked him to compare the morale of his team when his store announced position cuts but he didn't lose any.

"What makes it worth it for you?" I asked.

"My team. To see them succeed." He replied, feeling almost a sense of relief that he knew his role and purpose as a leader.

I nodded and agreed. "Feel pride in what you do to help your team grow, learn, and feel safe in the security of their job."

Leaders: Every effort you give in this business will come back to you ten-fold. You may not see it right away, but it is a build. Would you want to work for someone that felt their efforts were inconsequential? If you feel this way, no offense, but go home. You are putting all our jobs at risk as your lack of passion does more harm than good. Your job is to inspire, motivate, and develop your team as you own your business.

SURVEY MONKEY YOUR LIFE

What do you want to be known for and how will you impact others in your lifetime?

What mark will be your personal legacy?

What is more important to you, doing the right thing or doing what you think other people think is right?

Before reading on, fill in those blanks and ask yourself two more questions:

1. What is a goal/or goals that I can work toward this month?

2. What is a goal/or goals I can work toward this year?

Did you write down very attainable and reachable goals? Nice! If you keep your eye on the prize and your focus matches your effort, then you are more than likely going to reach that goal,

I am confident of that. But now, I want you to think about the fire in your belly and stretch your dreams and goals to the highest they can go. The larger the aspirations, the bigger the accomplishments. Think BIG. Think outrageous. Then write it down. Now, let's put those thoughts into action. One thing to remember? Those small steps add up into one BIG accomplishment. Write down your goal and work towards your dreams one step at a time. No one is stopping you, and if they are, then I think you should rethink your relationship. Because we're not going for "nice" accomplishments, we're going for the distance. Period.

My very talented and entrepreneurial-thinking friend, Gina Centeno says, "If people say it is impossible, then it is impossible for them, not you." You only live once, and why spend that time on something you don't fully enjoy? As you reach for the stars, you will see walls start to come down, one brick at a time. Be aware, some people will not be happy for the success and accomplishments you achieve, but that is not your fault. Some will applaud you, and some will try and make you feel unworthy or even guilty. SHUT IT DOWN and do not listen or acknowledge it.

KICK IT INTO HIGH GEAR

I had a conversation with a friend, let's call her Elise, who started a new management position with a cosmetic company.

Elise was explaining how discouraged she was in her position of just over a year, a position she has worked her entire life for. Elise has had great success as a visionary and big picture activation within her organization and received several awards and recognition in the short period of time. I guess that is why I was surprised to hear a voice of defeat while she looked down at her coffee. Elise proceeded to explain to me that after recognition within her company, she started feeling guilty and unworthy. She was new and felt that her peers deserved to have the spotlight, not just her. She couldn't understand why she was singled out, while her experienced and very deserving co-workers were not.

"I didn't want to be recognized anymore. I love my position and want it to be long term. I am not a solo show and need the encouragement and support of my team. They taught me so much already and they deserve the recognition. Without them, I wouldn't have been as successful. I was feeling awkward and isolated, and I took a step back." she explained.

"What? What do you mean? You quit?!" I was in shock.

"No, I didn't quit. I just didn't drive myself the way I formerly did. I kind of 'took a breather,'" and shrugged her shoulders.

I nodded my head and truly was in disbelief. Why would someone want to sacrifice their own growth and feel that was the way to empower her co-workers? I tried to hide my emotion that she was acting ridiculous, but I don't have the best poker face.

She saw it and said, "Ugh. I know what you are thinking, and I am ashamed. I felt ashamed getting recognition, and now I feel ashamed not getting recognition because my business suffered as a result. I stopped being creative and innovative. I don't know what feels worse."

"Ok, let me get this straight." I put my coffee down, as I tend to talk with my hands (the Italian side comes out when I feel passionate). "I think you need to give yourself a break. You have taken on everyone's emotions and feel responsible to make everyone happy. You will NEVER make everyone happy. If something works, some people still may not like the way it works. If something doesn't work, some people won't like that as well. It is your responsibility to work for your team to the best of your ability."

I continued, "Everyone has a moment where they shine more than others and you were having that. In this time in retail, take it and RUN. Any time you or your co-workers succeed or fail as a result of effort, everyone elevates. FAILURES and SUCCESSES equal growth if there are learnings from it. SEDENTARY equals decline. Being a great co-worker doesn't mean taking a back seat, it means having courage to move forward with ideas and new ways of trying things. You were having a moment and there is nothing wrong with that. You must get that drive back, now on an uphill battle, to really contribute and add value to your team and co-workers."

As my mentor would say, "Sometimes you are the big shit, and other times the little ca-ca." The phrase cut the seriousness, and Elise perked up. She chuckled and nodded. "Ok, Becky. You made your point. I better get to work."

You are a Beauty Boss. Speak up and never put yourself in the backseat. Your voice matters.

9

THE GIFT OF TIME

———

Time goes whether we like it or not. My ultimate goal for you is to never want time to "go by fast" in any sense of your life. How we spend it directly impacts our success and happiness. Deliberate presence in each moment takes effort and discipline as life will pass in a blink of an eye. Time deserves respect, awareness, and a certain amount of fearlessness to balance it on your terms. Discipline requires the absence of distraction to ensure efficiency and fluidity.

MASTER THE SCHEDULE

A person's schedule is their livelihood. It dictates when they will have time for family and friends or any other personal activity. Daycare costs, weekend baseball games, and holidays are just a few examples of how a schedule impacts life. For some companies, there is a tough balance of accommodating people while focusing on the needs of the business.

If there are specific scheduling expectations of a position, they should be given on or before the interviewing process. It is also the candidates' responsibility to ask the appropriate questions to avoid any potential issues.

A certain amount of flexibility on both sides is needed, but if there is not enough staff during busy "must win" times, business will suffer, and jobs will be at risk. Keeping that in mind, *showing up* to work on time and ready to go is one of the most important responsibilities as an employee. Your job should be important enough that you are scheduled and working because you give VALUE. If you think it doesn't make a difference whether you are late or miss a shift altogether, then it is time to rethink the value of your contributions. Life happens and there will be times where you may miss work on occasion, but just be aware that full participation defines your dependability, reliability, value, and reputation.

Leaders: Consistency and fairness is key. Even if a schedule is auto-computer generated, do not wash your hands of the situation. You need an opinion as a business driver and team leader. It is your responsibility to do what is best for the business while doing what is best for your people. Speak up.

FOLLOW THROUGH ON YOUR FOLLOW-UP

I am not a fan of leaving business up to "chance." Strategize on what actions to take to promote business. If you rely on chance, or if it's busy, then there is no way to generate sustainable and consistent sales performance. I believe in offering services or products to anyone and everyone, because if you do not offer, then you are making the decision for them to not try it. Keep yourself visible and active in every way possible, and when business may be tough, this is the time to try even harder. Do not get comfortable, relax, or give up. Never give up.

About a year after I had the twins, I could not work more than six hours a week and my only available day was Monday. Needless to say, in a retail world, this is less than ideal. Fortunately, I had a very strong reputation and Nordstrom hired me for six hours every Monday from 3 to 9 pm. My husband and I were financially strained, and these six hours meant more than you could know. I knew I was lucky to be given these hours, but also realized that I needed to provide my value in order to keep them. I was given a non-negotiable SPH (sales per hour) goal, just like everyone else.

I am confident of my selling skills; however I am not a magician. 3 to 9 pm on a Monday is typically a ghost town. I had no existing clientele since this was my first time back in more than a year. Desperate to make it work, I asked my cosmetic department manager, whom I respected very much, for advice.

Lorene Losher was the best department manager I have ever worked for. She was tough as nails and her expectations were incredibly high. People wanted to succeed for her, and sometimes despite her, but nonetheless people who worked for her wanted to WIN. When reunited with co-workers from those days, we laugh about how we worked our tails off for Lorene's initiatives and department goals to the point of exhaustion. We also remember the pride felt of achieving goals that initially were viewed as impossible, and it brought us to tears as a team. Proud tears. Happy Tears. Exhausted tears. And as much as we questioned why we were putting ourselves through this agony of making sure that results were delivered just as Lorene expected, the camaraderie of conquering what we set out to do fed our souls enough to endure it again and again. There was no greater feeling of winning, not just for her, but for us. Lorene knew exactly what she was doing, and we loved her for it.

Knowing that disappointing Lorene was not an option, I asked her for advice.

"Ummmm... Lorene?" I said in a little squeaky voice. "I am not sure how I am going to make my hourly goals on Monday nights." I looked down, shaking my head.

You would assume that a manager would suggest opening their availability and working a more productive time, but instead she said, "Becky, this is what you are going to do. You will see at least one customer a week. You are going to make a connection with that one customer, even if all you do is suggest a product or sample. Let them know that you will follow up next week and write them a thank you note immediately after they leave. That next week follow up with them and repeat these steps every single week like clockwork. You will build a successful clientele and business. All you have to do is follow through on what you promise."

Follow through on what I promise? That's easy.

I did just as she said. I made sure that I treated everyone as though they were a gift and built relationships one week at a time and one person at a time. I didn't need magic, I just needed to make sure I did my job, offering what we had available and not take my knowledge for granted. One year later, and every year for eight years, I produced as much as a full-time employee, working only six hours a week.

Do not let roadblocks get in your way. Be solution-minded and when you don't have the solution, ask for help! Giving up is not an option and neither are excuses. Coincidentally, another moment I will never forget is when I did not achieve a goal for one of our department "MUST WIN" events.

"How did you do today, Becky?" Lorene asked at the end of the night. I looked down at my feet and told her I didn't make my goal. I felt like I let myself and everyone down.

"You can't hit a homerun every time, ya know," she said curtly, turned around, and kept walking.

Little did she know, that day she taught me to give myself grace. I picked myself up and realized that even though I didn't hit that home run, I sure as hell tried.

Give it all you've got, go for it, and feel proud of doing the best you can. Grant yourself grace and Never. Give. Up.

NO EXCUSES

I hear specific reasons why people don't follow up. I don't want to bother them. They don't buy anything anyway. It isn't a good time to call because they are all eating dinner. They are probably on vacation. It is a waste of time because they never answer me. I'm limited to my follow up methods. I reach out to them too much, and they are going to stop shopping with me because I will annoy them. It goes on and on, so let me help you out.

By not following up with customers, you are leaving business to happen by chance. It is a roll of the dice and you leave all control up to how the wind will blow on that particular day. The most successful people in this industry have a clientele base. When you meet a customer and either close out the sale, have a conversation, or ring them up, the best thing to do is be honest with what your customer can expect from you. I like to call this "under promise and over deliver." If they do not want to be contacted, do not take it personally. Let them know the ways they can self-navigate staying informed either digitally or in person.

Want to see your business soar? *Follow through on your follow up.* Keep calling/texting (appropriately) until people tell you not to. You are doing your job by informing customers of what they requested. If you feel that you may be informing your connections too often, just ask them their preferences. There is no need to hold your breath as you make a phone call or text message. If you are unsure when or how people like to be contacted, ASK THEM, they are PEOPLE and it is ok for anyone to say yes or no.

KNOW YOUR MUST WIN MONTHS AND WORK HARD, THEN TAKE TIME OFF TO RECHARGE

A realtor will have "peak months" to sell houses. The time to make the most money is the start of spring, usually beginning of February through the end of June. Not only does the weather start to improve, but families prefer to move before summer and fall when a new school year begins. It always depends on how hot the market is, but usually this is the time to hustle hard and ensure the financial stability for the year.

This is the same in retail/sales. There are the busy seasons that you absolutely MUST WIN to make sure it solidifies the budget and job security for the rest of the year. If a specific must win season isn't met, it is almost impossible to dig out of that hole. It is an uphill battle that you would rather plan strategically for and start off great out of the gate. A strong start is a precursor to a strong season. A must win season is more important than ever to get your commitment in check. This is going to make or break business goals and everyone has to participate one hundred percent.

What does full participation mean? It means doing everything possible to pull your weight and achieve your goals. The minute you don't achieve a personal sales goal, someone on your team must achieve their personal goal, and also make up for what is left on the table. How can I say this lightly? If you do not achieve your sales goal you are putting your job and others at risk. If you feel like for some reason you cannot achieve a goal, ask for help. People want you to succeed, but it is essential that you care enough about your personal results.

January is a completely different environment than the month prior. Black Friday seems like a million years ago and it is the start of the new year. The hustle and bustle of shoppers has traded itself in for quiet footsteps and there is a hodge-podge of holiday items leftover as spring merchandise comes in. In other words, "it's slow". Events are sprinkled in to generate buzz and people into stores, but on most days in January, it's quiet for retail. A couple of things may happen in January. My suggestion is to go on a little getaway or take a few days off to recover from the busiest time of year. For others, many people quit after the holiday season because it was either too physically demanding, difficulty balancing quality time with their family, or exhaustion from the extended work hours. It is not a known statistic, but I have personally seen the most turnover during this month.

Beginners: Feeling exhausted from the holiday season is completely normal. Usually, 60 percent of business is done though those crucial months, and be grateful people are shopping! Don't quit because of this. Things go back to a bit of a slower pace where you can use your creativity to generate business and commit to new goals or challenges during the year. You have a year under your belt and the balance gets easier as you realize what is expected. Feel accomplished and reflect on amazing encounters and relationships you have developed over this time. Hang in there!!!!

Seasoned: Congrats on surviving another holiday season!!! You are an inspiration and the positivity you show throughout the long hours gives others the "I can do this, too" attitude. Sometimes you think how many more of these can I do, but then you remember how you felt as a "beginner" and realize this is your "reflect and reset" time. Take this time and set new goals as the retail footprints change and challenge yourself to really embrace new tools introduced.

Leaders: This is one of the most important times to inspire and motivate your teams. Celebrate and recognize the work your team has endured. Write them a personal little note in appreciation, it will go a longer way than you think. Be aware of morale in your store/department and keep everyone energized as the new year begins. Your energy and excitement are contagious!!! Reminder: If you see any of your employees unengaged after a busier time of the year has ended, try and challenge them with more responsibility or an event to plan. This will keep them engaged and less likely to look elsewhere. Extra responsibility also platforms your employees for personal and professional growth. Do a temperature check on your team to make sure everyone feels that they are in a good place. Reset and ask individuals what their personal goals are for the new year. *Your sincere and authentic personal interest for your team is always crucial.*

10

PRACTICE WHAT YOU PREACH: SELF CARE 101

───

It is ironic (and typical) how I saved the "self-care" chapter for last. Safety and self-care is the most important chapter in this book. Anyone in the service industry caters to everyone else before we "service" ourselves. After we complete our day of work, we return home to take care of our kids, spouse, pets, and friends. It is our nature to take care of people, and our personal needs take a back burner. When YOU are taken care of, the world is a better place. This is not up to anyone but ourselves.

Do not rely on anyone else to fully meet your physical or emotional needs because at the end of the day, we are the only ones that truly know what they are. Your health is your most important job. The result is a happier, healthier, higher-performing YOU. You cannot take care of anyone properly if you do not take care of yourself first.

LISTEN TO YOUR GUT, LITERALLY

I learned quickly when I needed to take my health seriously. Many of you are thinking, "Yeah, right. Like I have time for myself. Next chapter, please." I get it. You are busy. And if you have not experienced the type of busy yet where suddenly your life gets placed in the back seat (or so far back you are hanging onto the bumper…being dragged on the ground while the car is pushing 90 mph) remember this story:

After my daughter Adriana was born in 2010, I had three children under the age of three. Between a baby and twin two-year-old boys, Noah and Patrick, I was exhausted to the point that my voice slurred when I spoke (no cocktails needed). Quality sleep or quiet time seemed like a distant memory. The only time I sat down to eat was when I worked on Monday nights. Once a week, I would take a thirty-minute break, go to a "fast" restaurant in the mall, and eat a personal size cheese pizza. It was my own slice of heaven as I sat in that booth quietly and just relaxed. Little did I know, it was making me sick….

Over the next six months, I became weaker and very frail. I am a very high-strung person as it is, and at that point in time, my anxiety was through the roof. The boys were born premature, and at almost three years old and they were not talking. They only spoke gibberish to one another, and I enrolled them in an early intervention speech therapy that my county offered. Patrick had asthma from underdeveloped lungs and ER trips for breathing treatments in the middle of the night were not uncommon. This was also when he did this awful "head banging" habit every time I couldn't understand what he was trying to communicate. He literally got on all fours, and then slammed his head on the ground. Just thinking about it makes my knees weak to this day.

Each morning I woke up with my stomach in knots and had a permanent stomachache. Every single day for six months, I was unable to normally digest any food until 2 pm. Thank goodness I knew to drink a ton of water to prevent dehydration. Over the months I made a few doctor's appointments but then canceled because I was too busy, or felt fine enough for the moment and saw it as unnecessary.

As money was more than tight, I tried to enroll my twins in the preschool program through the public school where the fees would be waived due to their speech therapy needs. We packed up and walked to the elementary school for the preschool assessment. This would determine if they would be placed on the high priority list of children that "need" the "free school program". Once we arrived at the assessment, the boys had to be split up to see how they interacted separately with the teachers. I lived in a baby cave and they were never split up. One was a head banger. They still had pacifiers and would scream without them... then the teachers wanted to test their fine motor skills by giving them scissors. Scissors??? I was supposed to teach my twin toddlers how to use scissors?! I set up these poor boys to fail miserably!

One of the teachers that evaluated the boys called a few hours later that same day. She explained to me her concerns about the boys and that she did not believe that they could properly interact with other children normally. I asked her if they would be able to interact with the other children at the first t-ball class that started the next week, and she said flatly, no. I told her she was wrong and could not tell me about my children after one hour of being with them. Ohhhhh, my stomach....

That next week, my husband and I packed the stroller with Adriana and took the boys to their first t-ball class. The parents sat on the perimeter of the elementary school gym while the coach took attendance of the three-year-old players that were instructed to sit in the middle of the gym. The coach took attendance and had the tiny players say their name and favorite food. After my husband finally got Patrick and Noah out of the bathroom where they were entranced with the automatic hand dryers, they proceeded to the gym. The boys were the only children running in circles while attendance was taken, like crazy wild horses that have been caged their whole lives.

It was a scene. They were screaming and laughing while I was trying to catch TWO three-year-olds running around this huge gym. All the parents were watching this show while my poor husband stood there next to the stroller like a deer in headlights as he was frozen in terror and shock. Literally, I think he blacked out! As I was running after them, my one flip flop broke, and I started running with one shoe. I finally lassoed them in and we called it a day at t-ball. I can laugh about it now. Cry and laugh actually, but at the time? I just knew that my stomach hurt.

I ran into a neighbor a few days later that happens to be a twin. I told her the stories between the preschool evaluations and the t-ball incident. She said, "Why don't you just enroll them in Small Miracles Preschool down the street? They will do amazing there, it is a wonderful school. Go check it out."

The director of the private preschool, Brenda Hoppestad, gave us a window of time that class was in session. I packed, and headed over. When we walked in, there were about a dozen three-year-old children at tables eating a snack. Brenda set two extra spots anticipating our visit, and the boys sat down. They immediately started eating and pleasantly interacting with the other children while I stood in the back of the classroom with happy tears streaming down my face. Brenda, you will never know what that day meant to me.

That night I was exhausted. I told Tim, my husband, that I was too tired to walk up the stairs to bed. Literally, I was too tired. He carried me up and told me he could see how run down I was.

Tim was concerned. I reassured him that I was fine and there was nothing to worry about.

A week later I went to work, and before I went on my 30-minute relaxing pizza break, a co-worker Mariam came up to me and ran her hand down my back. She looked at me and said, "There is something wrong. I see your bones. Are you ok?" I told her I was exhausted to the point my husband carried me up the stairs. I have three young children with a nervous stomach. She shook her head and repeated, "Becky, there is something wrong."

I finally went to the doctor the next day. Turned out I had a chronic stomach infection and ended up with recurrent salmonella poisoning. It also turned out that I am highly sensitive to gluten and those pizzas every week were making it worse. I hadn't been properly digesting food for six months and was malnourished. I was lucky to be functioning.

Mariam opened my eyes that something was seriously wrong with my health and saved my life that day. Another angel on Earth that I will never forget. It was a long recovery, but I am forever grateful to get the chance.

Never procrastinate taking care of yourself. Do not cancel appointments that are needed for your health because you are too busy, or something came up. Do everything in your power to take care of yourself FIRST. Find the time to eat healthy, workout, and stay focused on your physical and mental well-being. Nothing is worth putting your health in the back seat.

IT WILL BE BETTER THAN OK

When I look back at the most stressful times of my life, I wish I heard a voice telling me, "things will be ok." I feel that if I had stopped worrying as much, I could have just enjoyed moments and live in the present. While I absolutely assure you that things will be ok for you, I also want you to know that it will be better than that.

You are destined to make an impact.

Letting go of control was one of the hardest things I've ever done. It was also the most freeing. I actually had to train my brain to stop worrying and live in the moment. I had to train my brain to stop being nervous all the time, for whatever the reason might have been. I trained my brain to start listening to people when they spoke rather than thinking about what I was going to say next. Practice letting go of what you cannot control and change the channel in your brain. Storms will pass and sometimes they will purposely force us to slow down to live a bit simpler.

Stop worrying yourself to the point where you get sick because difficult times are *moments in time*. Take time to care and invest in yourself because you are too important to so many people.

A few last words of advice from my heart to yours. Do your best, whatever that best will be at the time. Give yourself a break. Slow down. Have integrity and be the person you are meant to be. Look in the mirror - really look at yourself. Health radiates from the inside out. Make sure that when it's bedtime, you can reflect on the day and remember you did *something* significant. Serve others and do not be self-serving.

Find what feeds your soul and Never. Give. Up. Make an impact. I believe in you.

#IMPACT

ABOUT THE AUTHOR

Becky Feeley is a twenty-year veteran of the luxury cosmetic, skincare, and fragrance industry. She started her career in department store leadership and transitioned into the world of beauty where she had many roles ranging from Beauty Advisor to Cosmetic Executive. After two decades of cosmetic retail experience, Becky is known as a forward, solution oriented, and strategic thinker that innovates through action. Struggles with infertility, financial hardship, and surviving a brain tumor has shaped her life, and she believes the power of beauty is more than just skin deep. Becky trusts that hard work will always pay off, and deliberate presence in each moment will help find purpose and fulfillment in life.

www.ingramcontent.com/pod-product-compliance
Lightning Source LLC
Chambersburg PA
CBHW060445040426
42331CB00044B/2627